Minnesota
Wildflowers

A children's
field guide to
the state's most
common flowers

Interpreting the Great Outdoors

Text by Beverly Magley, Illustrations by DD Dowden

For cousin Joey
love, Bevy

&

In loving memory of Russ Dowden
(1922-1991)

Interpreting the Great Outdoors

Nature's wonders, such as the wildflowers, are certainly remarkable, but unfortunately many people—especially young people—know little about them. That's one reason Falcon Press has launched this series of books called Interpreting the Great Outdoors.

Other books in the series include *The Tree Giants: The Story of the Redwoods, the World's Largest Trees; The Fire Mountains: The Story of the Cascade Volcanoes; California Wildflowers; Arizona Wildflowers;* and *Oregon Wildflowers.*

To get extra copies of this book or others in the series, write to Falcon Press, P.O. Box 1718, Helena, MT 59624. Or call toll-free 1-800-582-2665. Falcon Press publishes and distributes a wide variety of books and calendars, so be sure to ask for our free catalog.

Copyright © 1992
by Falcon Press Publishing Co., Inc.,
Billings and Helena, Montana.

Botanical consultants: Bonnie Harper-Lore and Maria Urice, Midwest Regional Office, National Wildflower Research Center.

On the cover: Blueberry, Trillium, and Showy Lady Slipper (the state flower).

Design, illustrations, editing, typesetting, and other prepress work by Falcon Press, Helena, Montana. Printed in Singapore.

Library of Congress Number 91-58877
ISBN 1-56044-117-8

Contents

Introduction

Zing! The brilliant yellow and deep red colors of a wildflower grab your attention. On bent knee to look more closely, you can sniff the flower's lovely fragrance and admire its beauty. While there, it's easy to notice more flowers, tiny and shy, tucked close to the earth. Their shiny green leaves have many shapes and sizes, and the world of flowering plants becomes more interesting. Some plants are just poking up through the ground. Others have tightly furled buds not yet ready to open. Still others are in full bloom.

Flowering plants have existed for about 120 million years. They evolved when dinosaurs roamed the earth. Flowers are unique because each of their seeds has a protective, nourishing shell that helps the seed survive.

The sweet nectar of wildflowers entices nectar-eaters that pollinate the flowers. The pollinated blossoms then produce seeds. A nice trade! So when you see a bee or an ant crawling inside a flower or watch a hummingbird or butterfly sip nectar, remember they are essential to the survival of flowers. The blossoms also provide shelter for insects and other little creatures.

Minnesota has about 1,800 species of flowering plants. Most of these flowers have adapted to Minnesota's specific conditions: its soggy wetlands, dry windy prairies, or shady forests. This book features native wildflowers that have grown here for hundreds or thousands of years (unless otherwise noted). A native Minnesota wildflower is one that has existed here since before European settlement of the area.

Lie on your back and look at a flower as it splashes color up to the sky. Turn onto your side and get an ant's-eye view of the world. Then go belly-down to see how many different plants are growing right under your nose. It's amazing!

I will be the gladdest thing under the sun!
I will touch a hundred flowers and not pick one.

Edna St. Vincent Millay
"Afternoon on a Hill"

Wetlands, Lakes, and Rivers

Sploosh! splash! You might have to get your feet wet to see the flowers that grow here. Many plants can grow with their roots entirely submerged, while their leaves and flowers float on the water's surface. Bogs provide so few nutrients that some of the plants that grow in them have learned to digest insects. Flowing water and muddy banks provide abundant moisture for other water-loving flowers. These flowers live in the company of otters and beavers and brighten the way for many animals who come to the water for a drink.

Broad-Leaved Arrowhead

other names: Duck Potato
height: 1 to 2 feet
season: July to September

Inconspicuous female flowers hide below the showy male blossoms, awaiting the falling pollen. The leaves are usually shaped like arrowheads, but when the plant grows in a strong current, the leaves look like long streamers. Ducks and muskrats eat the roots. Indians taught early settlers to roast and eat the roots, too.

Sagittaria latifolia

Marsh Marigold

other names: Cowslip
height: 1 to 2 feet
season: April to June

These water-loving plants grow in boggy areas. The stems and undersides of the leaves are tinged with purple, and the pretty white blossoms have bright yellow anthers in their centers. The plant's scientific name describes the blossom: the Greek word *kalthos* means "cup"; the Latin word *palustris* means "of the swamp." The steamed leaves taste a bit like spinach, and some people pickle the buds and eat them.

Caltha palustris

Skunk Cabbage

other names: none
height: 4 to 6 inches
season: February to May

Tiny greenish-yellow freckles dot the purple spathe. A spathe is a shell-like leaf that covers the spadix, an unusual knob covered with tiny flowers. The spathe of this plant smells a bit skunky when injured. Little ridges on the roots pull the plant close to the ground each spring to keep the leaves and flower buds away from cold winds.

Symplocarpus foetidus

Spotted Touch-Me-Not

Yellow Pond Lily

Pickerel Weed

other names: none
height: 1 to 2 feet above surface
  of water
season: June to November

Pickerels and other freshwater
fish often swim and lay eggs
where pickerel weeds grow.
Ducks like to eat the seeds and
roots of this plant. The stem has
a number of little air compart-
ments that help the plant float
and keep its spike of flowers
above water level. Each blossom
opens for just one day.

*Pontederia
cordata*

other names: Jewel Weed,
  Snapweed
height: 2 to 3 feet
season: July to October

Hummingbirds can reach
the nectar hidden deep in the
blossom, but some smart
bumblebees drill a little hole
at the back to get at the
sweet treat. After this plant
blossoms, a more appropriate
name might be "touch-me-
please." The ripe seedpods
pop open at the tiniest touch
and fling out their seeds. So
touching this plant gently actually helps it to distribute
seeds that will grow next
year.

Impatiens capensis

other names: Bullhead Lily
height: floats on the water
season: May to September

Heart-shaped leaves float on
the surface of a calm pond,
while the yellow cup-shaped
flowers reach just above the
water's surface. To survive in
water, the plant brings air
down the hollow stems of
young leaves and then returns
it up the stems of older leaves.
Indians roasted the seeds like
popcorn or ground them into
flour for breads.

Nuphar luteum subsp.
variegatum

Round-Leaved Sundew

other names: none
height: 4 to 9 inches
season: June to August

Sundew leaves look like round green suns with little shiny rays. When insects investigate this plant, the leaf hairs fold over and the bug gets stuck in goo. The sundew takes several days to suck the nutritious juices from an insect. Then the leaf opens up, and the bug skeleton dries up and blows away.

Drosera rotundifolia

Pitcher Plant

other names: Trumpet
height: 8 to 24 inches
season: May to August

Sweet nectar on the edge of the pitcher-shaped leaf entices insects. A bug can easily crawl down the tube, but tiny barbed, downward-pointing hairs on the inside of the leaf prevent it from climbing back out. When the insect falls into the bottom of the "pitcher," plant fluids and bacteria digest the unlucky critter.

Sarracenia purpurea

Calla Lily

other names: Water Calla, Water Arum
height: 4 to 8 inches
season: June to July

The spathe is like a white banner enfolding the yellow flowers on the spadix. These tiny flowers turn into clusters of bright red berries in late summer. The scientific name *palustris* means "of marshes." The calla lily only grows in wet areas. Look for this plant in northern Minnesota.

Calla palustris

Cattail

other names: none
height: 3 to 9 feet
season: May to July

Ever had a cattail pancake? Indians used every part of this plant. The pollen makes a flour for pancakes, breads, or cakes. The leaves can be woven into baskets. The downy seeds are good insulation and make good pillow stuffing or absorbent padding for diapers. The roots are edible.

Typha latifolia

Stinging Nettle

other names: none
height: 2 to 4 feet
season: June to September

Ouch! Like syringes, the tiny needles under each leaf poke your skin and shoot in a stinging juice. (The sting goes away after a while.) Like most nettles, these are edible and high in protein. Cooking the young plant eliminates the sting, but wear gloves to pick it. The scientific name *urtica* comes from a Latin word that means "to burn." The plant was brought here from Europe.

Urtica dioica

Wild Iris

other names: Blue Flag
height: 2 to 3 feet
season: May to August

Iris was the Greek goddess of the rainbow. In this plant, rainbow colors appear in the center of the petals. In some cultures, the three petals symbolize faith, wisdom, and courage, and in Europe a carved iris was often placed at the top of a queen's or king's scepter. American Indians twisted the silky leaf fibers into rope for hunting and fishing.

Iris versicolor

Woodlands

Minnesota has lots of trees. The northern forests are composed mostly of pines, firs, spruces, and other evergreens. Other woodlands throughout the state are primarily deciduous. That means the trees grow new leaves each spring and drop them every autumn.

Some wildflowers live in the dense shade and shelter of a thick forest, while other flowers prefer the open forest floor or a sunny meadow. Watch for a shy deer here. Listen for the creak of two trees rubbing against each other. Notice the birds singing and calling. Sit and watch red or gray squirrels dash up and down their tree homes.

Wood Lily

other names: Prairie Lily, Orange Cup, Flame Lily
height: 1 to 3 feet
season: June to August

Bright reddish-orange flowers have a golden throat and purple freckles. Lilies were the sacred flower of motherhood to the ancient Greeks and Romans. Today, many varieties of lilies are grown by gardeners and florists. Most familiar is the Easter lily, originally brought to the United States from China.

Lilium philadelphicum

Jack-in-the-Pulpit

other names: Indian Turnip
height: 1 to 3 feet
season: April to June

Some people think this plant looks like a preacher standing in a fancy, old-fashioned covered pulpit. the striped spathe forms a little roof to protect the flowering spadix. Gently lift the spathe: the plant is female if the flowers look like tiny green berries. If the flowers have little thread-like stamen and are dropping pollen, the plant is male. Insects fly from plant to plant and spread the pollen. Indians cooked and ate the corm of this plant.

Arisaema triphyllum

Dutchman's Breeches

other names: Blue Staggers
height: 4 to 12 inches
season: April to May

Two puffy spurs joined at the bottom look like an old-fashioned pair of britches hanging upside-down on a clothesline. The other common name refers to the behavior of cattle if they eat this toxic plant.

Dicentra cucullaria

Solomon's Seal

other names: Smooth Solomon's Seal
height: 8 inches to 3 feet
season: May to June

When the stalk breaks away from the rhizome, it leaves a scar that some people think looks like the official seal of King Solomon of olden days. Maybe yes—and maybe not. But the plant's scientific name describes it well: *polygonum* means "many knees" and refers to the little swellings at each leaf node. Indians taught early settlers to eat the starchy rhizomes. The dangling yellowish flowers become hard green berries that turn dark blue in fall.

Polygonatum biflorum

Wood Anemone

other names: Windflower
height: 6 to 8 inches
season: April to June

Early peoples around the world associated this plant with the wind, perhaps because its slender stalks shiver in the slightest breeze. Native Americans called it the "flower of the wind," and its scientific name is derived from *Anemos*, the name of the Greek god of the wind.

Anemone quinquefolia

Columbine

other names: Honeysuckle
height: 1 to 2 feet
season: April to July

Hummingbirds use their long bills to sample the nectar of the columbine, but short, stubby bumblebees must drill holes in the spurs to get at the sweet prize. You might like the nectar, too. Columbine comes from the Latin word *columba*, meaning "dove." Can you see the five doves with their shared wings outspread?

Aquilegia canadensis

11

Woodlands continued

Lady Slipper

other names: Noah's Ark,
    Whippoorwill Shoe
height: 4 to 28 inches
season: May to July

A brilliantly colored lip petal forms a tiny ballet slipper complete with long, striped purple petals ready to tie around a tiny dancer's ankle. Bees are good at retrieving the nectar from this plant, but other insects get trapped inside by the curled lower lip. The white and pink Showy Lady Slipper is the state flower of Minnesota. It grows as tall as three feet.

Showy Lady Slipper
Cypripedium reginae

Yellow Lady Sliper
Cypripedium calceolus

Trillium

other names: Wake Robin
height: 8 to 18 inches
season: April to June

"Tri" in the name trillium means three, just as it does in the word triangle. This plant has three large green leaves, three white petals that turn pinkish with age, three sepals, three styles, and three reddish berries. Trillium has the common name wake robin, because it blooms early in spring—about when the first robins arrive. If you pick the bloom from a trillium, the plant may die or not bloom again for years.

Trillium grandiflorum

White Trout Lily

other names: White Dogtooth
    Violet, Adder's Tongue
height: 4 to 10 inches
season: April to June

Mottled brown splotches on the leaves look like the freckles on a brown trout. This lily's white flower petals are often tinged with lavender or pink. Black bears enjoy eating the dogtooth-shaped bulbs, and deer nibble the green seedpods.

Erythronium albidum

Wild Geranium

other names: Crane's Bill
height: 1 to 2 feet
season: April to June

Geranium is the Greek word for crane. The plant got its name because its fruit looks like the beak of a crane. If a fruit pod is ripe and still closed, touch it gently and watch the tiny cups fling seeds through the air.

*Geranium
maculatum*

Bellwort

other names: Wild Oat, Merrybell
height: 6 to 20 inches
season: April to June

Peer into someone's mouth and you can see their uvula, the little thing dangling at the back of the throat. People used to think this plant could cure throat problems, because the blossoms dangle down like our uvulas.

*Uvularia
grandiflora*

Wild Ginger Root

other names: Wild Ginger
height: 6 to 12 inches
season: April to May

You have to be very observant to spot a shy wild ginger blossom with its long, tapered petal-like bracts. The heart-shaped leaves are shiny, and the brownish flower lies close to the ground where it's easy to attract pollinators such as millipedes, gnats, and flies.

*Asarum
canadense*

Woodlands continued

Lily of the Valley

other names: Canada Mayflower
height: 2 to 6 inches
season: May to June

These tiny blossoms smell wonderful! Lily of the valley is the special flower for people born in May, and its bloom time is described by the scientific name *maianthemum*, which means "May flower." The bright green, heart-shaped leaves collect dew and raindrops that trickle down to water the roots. Clusters of bright, shiny red berries adorn this plant in autumn.

Maianthemum canadense

May Apple

other names: none
height: 12 to 18 inches
season: April to June

Its flower looks like an apple blossom, and it blooms in May. That's how this plant got the name May apple. The roots, leaves, and seeds are poisonous, but you can make the golden fruits into a flavorful jelly. Raccoons like to eat the fruit, too.

Podophyllum peltatum

Wild Blue Phlox

other names: Wood Phlox
height: 10 to 20 inches
season: April to June

The blossoms look like blue pinwheels and are most fragrant in the evenings. A narrow tube leads butterflies and other long-tongued flying insects to the nectar, but the sticky stem discourages crawling insects such as ants.

Phlox divaricata

Jacob's Ladder

other names: none
height: 8 to 16 inches
season: April to June

The paired leaflets climbing this stalk are arranged like steps on a ladder, and the Bible says that Jacob dreamed of a ladder to heaven. Perhaps the sky-blue flowers at the top of the ladder are the color of heavenly bells.

Polemonium reptans

White Baneberry

other names: Doll's Eye
height: 1 to 2 feet
season: May to June

White feathery flowers cluster atop the stem in springtime. Bane means poison or harm. This plant forms poisonous berries in late summer. The other common name describes the berry's appearance: the dark spot on the end of the white berry looks like the eye of an old-fashioned china doll.

Actaea pachypoda

Violet

other names: Yellow Violet,
    Blue Violet
height: 6 to 16 inches
season: May to June

There are more than 300 species of violets in the world, and they come in many colors. In Minnesota you can find blue, violet, yellow, and white violets. A small pouch behind the violet's lower petal has little guide lines on it to direct bees to the nectar. The leaves are high in vitamin C, and the blossoms can be made into candy, jelly, syrup, or tea.

Yellow Violet
Viola pubescens

Blue Violet
Viola soraria

15

Fireweed

other names: none
height: 2 to 6 feet
season: July to September

Fireweed is often the first plant to grow after a forest fire. It helps enrich the burned area so that other plants can move back in. The flower blooms from the bottom up, so you may see seedpods, flowers, and buds on one plant. The seeds can be carried long distances by their little parachute-like hairs.

Epilobium angustifolium

Zig-Zag Goldenrod

other names: Goldenrod
height: 4 to 30 inches
season: July to October

Some people believed that if you carried these plants around, you would find treasure in the earth. So they named it golden rod. Each goldenrod plant has ten to twenty dark gold flower heads. Indians used the plant in steam baths to help ease pain, and its Latin name *solidago* means "to heal."

Solidago flexicaulis

Spring Beauty

other names: Indian Potato, Groundnut
height: 6 to 12 inches
season: March to May

Look closely and you'll see thin pink lines and spots of yellow decorating this early spring flower. Native Americans ate the nutty-tasting corm, a thick underground base. Black bears dig for the corms in the spring. Moose, deer, and sheep eat the flowers and leaves. It's a wonder any are left to blossom!

Claytonia virginica

Prairies

Tallgrass prairies once covered southern and western Minnesota. Today, most of the land has been plowed and planted in crops. Look for prairie plants in cemeteries, along railroad tracks and country roads, and on steep bluffs. Prairie plants survive in spite of little moisture, high winds, full sun, and hot temperatures. While scouting for prairie wildflowers, listen for the song of the meadowlark. Watch for fragile butterflies, and enjoy the scampering ground squirrels and gophers.

Pasque Flower

other names: Wild Crocus
height: 2 to 16 inches
season: March to April

These early blossoms open even before the leaves have pushed out of the ground. In milder climates, this flower blooms around Passover, and we call it the French word for Passover, pasque. The long silver hairs of the seed head make it look like a furry little creature with hair in its eyes.

Anemone patens

Prairie Larkspur

other names: none
height: 1 to 3 feet
season: May to July

The spur at the base of each blossom is like the long hind claw on a lark's foot—a lark's spur. The plant's scientific name comes from a Greek tale that tells of a fisherman who died saving a dolphin. In gratitude, King Neptune transformed the man's body into a flower bud shaped liked a dolphin. The word *delphinium* is Greek for dolphin.

Delphinium virescens

Prairie Sage

other names: Cudweed, Wormwood, Sagewort, Mugwort
height: 1 to 3 feet
season: July to September

Sage was used by many Plains Indian tribes for religious and medicinal purposes. Some tribes called it "magic feather," or "mosquito smoke" for its repellent qualities. The people of England call it wormwood because a concoction of it may help to get rid of intestinal worms. Call it whatever you like, but remember its unmistakable fragrance after a rainstorm on the prairie—wonderful!

Artemisia ludoviciana

Prairies continued

Pussy Toes

other names: Everlasting, Ladies' Tobacco
height: 6 to 18 inches
season: May to July

Like furry little toes on a kitten, pussy toes invite you to touch them gently. The tiny flowers are hidden within the white, furry "toes," or bracts. Painted Lady butterflies often lay their eggs on the undersides of the leaves. Pussy toes' feathery seeds remind some people of butterfly antennae, hence the scientific name *antennaria*.

Antennaria spp.

Many-Flowered Aster

other names: Heath Aster
height: 8 to 24 inches
season: August to September

Numerous starburst-shaped flowers adorn this prairie plant. The Greek word *aster* means star, and it's the basis of many words, including astronomy, astrology, asterisk, asteroid, and astronaut. Most of the 600 species of asters are native to North America.

Aster ericoides

Wild Onion

other names: Prairie Onion
height: 12 to 16 inches
season: June to August

Delicate lavender blossoms droop in a cluster at the end of the stalk. The plant tastes like an onion, and the scientific name *allium* means "garlicky." Cows that graze wild onions give sour-tasting milk, but the plant helped to flavor the meals of Indians and early explorers such as Lewis and Clark.

Allium stellatum

Purple Prairie Clover

other names: none
height: 1 to 2 feet
season: June to August

A garland of magenta blossoms encircles a cone. The blossoming circle begins at the bottom and gradually moves upward. This plant has lots of protein, and wild animals and domestic livestock both love to eat it.

Petalostemum purpureum

Wild Bergamot

other names: Beebalm, Horsemint
height: 1 to 2 feet
season: July to September

Gently feel the stem of this plant. Mints have square stems. You can make a flavorful tea from the leaves. Indians used the plant medicinally, and deer and cattle like to eat it.

Monarda fistulosa

Butterfly Weed

other names: Orange Milkweed, Butterfly Milkweed, Pleurisy Root
height: 12 to 30 inches
season: June to September

Butterflies love the nectar in these clustered, bright orange blossoms. Monarch butterflies depend on milkweeds for food as they migrate south each year. Early peoples chewed the roots to treat lung problems and used the fluffy seeds to stuff pillows. Some people decorated their hats with the feathery seeds.

Asclepias tuberosa

19

Evening Primrose

other names: none
height: 2 to 5 feet
season: June to September

Each fragile yellow blossom unfolds in the evening, awaiting pollination by night-flying insects. If you see one open in the morning, perhaps it's still waiting for an insect. Some nocturnal moths sleep in the closed blossoms during the day. Look for their wings sticking out of the flower. This plant produces as many as 6,000 seeds, and goldfinches love to gobble them.

Oenothera biennis

Prairie Blazing Star

other names: none
height: 16 inches to 4 feet
season: July to September

These look like lavender exclamation points in a meadow. As many as 100 individual flowers cluster on each stiff, hairy stem. They bloom from the top of the stem down. Prairie blazing stars are used by many florists and were first gathered in Minnesota for propagation in nurseries.

Liatris pycnostachya

Oxeye Daisy

other names: none
height: 1 to 2 feet
season: June to August

In England, people called this flower a "day's eye" because it opens each day and closes at night. The outer white rays surround a yellow center. Look through a magnifying glass for a closeup of the hundreds of tiny yellow tubular florets packed into the center.

Chrysanthemum leucanthemum

Black-Eyed Susan

other names: Brown-Eyed Susan
height: 1 to 3 feet
season: June to October

The bright yellow-orange rays attract insects, which find nectar in the drab brown center disc of florets. This plant must prefer flying insects, because tiny barbs on the stems discourage crawling bugs.

Rudbeckia hirta

Beard Tongue

other names: Penstemon, Wild Foxglove, Canterbury Bells
height: 2 to 3 feet
season: May to June

Such a funny-faced flower! A beard of long yellowish hairs dangles from the lower lip of each tubular blossom, while the upper lip has what looks like two tiny teeth projecting forward. Hummingbirds and insects with long mouth parts love to feed on the sweet nectar secreted deep inside the flower.

Penstemon grandiflorus

Wild Rose

other names: Prairie Wild Rose
height: 1 to 3 feet
season: June to July

Rose bushes provide food and cover for wildlife such as pheasants, grouse, quail, and black bears. People like the small pinkish fruit called a rosehip. Rosehips are so high in vitamin C that they are used to make vitamin tablets.

Rosa spp.

Prairies continued

other names: Widow's Tear, Blue
  Jacket, Cow Slobber
height: 8 inches to 2 feet
season: April to July

The arching leaves look like
the splayed legs of a spider.
Spiderwort's delicate flowers
bloom in the morning. By
afternoon, they turn into
jellylike blobs. This plant is
especially sensitive to
radiation and may help warn
us of dangerous pollution.

Blue-Eyed Grass

other names: none
height: 3 to 12 inches
season: May to June

The leaves looks like grass,
but this plant actually is a
member of the iris family.
Each blossom lasts only a
day, but the plant puts out
one after another and attracts
bees over a long growing
season. The scientific
name *sisyrinchium*
comes from a Greek
word meaning "pig
snout." Pigs love to root
in the ground
and eat the bulb.

Bluebell

other names: Harebell
height: 6 to 20 inches
season: June to September

The miniature blue bell-
shaped blossoms may be
tinged with pink or white.
The plant's scientific name
campanula is Latin for "little
bell." Blue is a traditional
color for hope—the color of
the sky in fine weather.

Campanula rotundifolia

Tradescantia bracteata

*Sisyrinchium
campestre*

Lead Plant

other names: none
height: 1 to 3 feet
season: May to July

White hairs on the leaves make the plant look a leaden gray. Indians used the leaves to make tea or smoked them like tobacco. The blossoms are interesting. Each has only one petal, and the gaudy yellow-orange stamen sticks right out.

Amorpha canescens

Thimbleweed

other names: Summer Anemone
height: 2 to 3 feet
season: June to August

Greenish or white flowers rise high above the leaves. The plant's fruit forms into a thimble-shaped cluster and provides the common name. One ancient myth tells that Venus cried about the death of Adonis, and each teardrop blossomed into an anemone.

*Anemone
cylindrica*

Yarrow

other names: none
height: 1 to 3 feet
season: June to September

Yarrow is very aromatic and has many medicinal uses. The scienific name, *Achillea millefolium,* was chosen because the famous Greek hero Achilles used it to treat his wounded soldiers. Properly prepared, yarrow can help stop bleeding, increase perspiration and break a fever, and ease a rash. The species is not native to Minnesota.

Achillea millefolium

23

Roadside and Disturbed Areas

People have a way of disrupting natural plant communities. We bulldoze roads, dig ditches, build railroads, and make trails. We build homes and plant garden flowers that go to seed and sprout up somewhere else. Sometimes fires burn an area or a flooding river rushes through.

All these disturbances create unique conditions that many plants find too harsh. But some plants, often thought of as weeds, are able to grow and flourish. Many of these plants are an important part of nature because they stabilize the soil with their roots, add needed nutrients, and prepare the way for grasses, shrubs, and trees to grow in the disturbed area again someday.

None of these plants is native to Minnesota.

Dandelion

other names: none
height: 2 to 18 inches
season: March to September

Hungry bumblebees love the nectar of dandelions. Our word dandelion comes from the French words *dent de lion,* which mean "teeth of the lion." Look for the five little teeth at the outside edge of each yellow floret, and at the toothlike leaves. Dandelions may be the world's most widespread and useful flowers. The leaves, roots, and flowers are edible and contain calcium and vitamins. Some people remove warts by putting the milky juice from the stem on them.

Taraxacum officinale

Queen Anne's Lace

other names: Wild Carrot
height: 1 to 3 feet
season: May to October

In the 1700s, Queen Anne of England wore this pretty plant instead of cloth lace. The central pinkish flower might be a drop of blood from her finger, pricked while sewing the plant to her collar. This is an ancestor of today's garden carrot.

Daucus carota

Chicory

other names: Blue Sailor
height: 1 to 4 feet
season: June to October

Try a science experiment with this flower: knock gently on an anthill with a stick until the ants come scurrying out. Hold the blue chicory blossom near the ants, and watch them shoot up formic acid to defend their mound. The blossom acts like natural litmus paper and turns pink where it is hit by the acid.

Cichorium intybus

Butter and Eggs

other names: Toadflax
height: 1 to 3 feet
season: May to October

The blossoms are gold and yellow, like an egg yolk in a pan of butter. The other common name is toadflax. Squeeze a blossom gently from the sides and watch it open like a toad's mouth. The juice from the leaves may stop the itch of your mosquito bites.

Linaria vulgaris

Mullein

other names: Flannel Mullein, Aaron's Road, Woolly Mullein
height: 3 to 6 feet
season: June to September

In its first year, this plant grows only a soft, fuzzy rosette of leaves. The starburst-shaped leaf hairs grow so densely that the whole plant appears woolly. The second year, a tall stalk emerges, and yellow blossoms cluster around the top. Ancient Romans and Greeks dipped the tall stalks in tallow to make torches.

Verbascum thapsus

Bindweed

other names: Wild Morning Glory
height: twining stems may be several feet long
season: June to August

This fast-growing vine can grow in a full circle around something in just two hours. The scientific name *convolvo* means "to entwine." The blossom is unusual because the pistils and pollen are white instead of the usual yellow of most flowers. The leaves have medicinal uses, and the taproot can grow as deep as ten feet into the ground.

Convolvulus spp.

Berries

Many plants produce berries after their flowers are fertilized. Some berries are delicious, while others are poisonous. Never eat a berry unless you're positive it's safe. And watch out for poison ivy while traipsing through the fields and woods looking for yummy, edible berries.

The soft pulp of a berry provides protection and nourishment for the seed enclosed within. Birds and animals eat the berries, leaves, stems, and even roots. People also use many parts of berry plants for food, medicines, and dyes. No wonder so many berry bushes have thorns! They need some protection against overuse.

All of these berries are native to Minnesota.

Blueberry

other names: Low Bush Blueberry
height: 8 to 12 inches
season: May to June for blossoms, June to July for berries

Blueberries might just have the best flavor of any berry in the entire world. Animals think so, too. Blueberries are a staple food for black bears, bobwhites, prairie chickens, ruffed grouse, and many other birds and mammals. Blueberries thrive on acidic soil and bright sunshine, and so Indians used to set fires to clear the land so that more blueberries would grow.

Vaccinium angustifolium

Strawberry

other names: none
height: 3 to 6 inches
season: April to June for blossoms, May to July for berries

Don't forget where you see the pretty white five-petaled blossoms of the strawberry so that you can return later to savor the sweet wild berries. Yum! Birds, turtles, small rodents, and bears also enjoy eating them. This plant got its name because many people lay straw under garden strawberries to keep them from rotting on wet ground.

Fragaria virginiana

Gooseberry

other names: none
height: 2 to 5 feet
season: May to June for blossoms, July to August for berries

The greenish-white flowers become burgundy-colored berries in late summer. Ripe gooseberries make wonderful pies and preserves, but it's hard to eat the berries plain without puckering your mouth. Some people brew the leaves to make a medicinal tea.

Ribes cynosbati

Thimbleberry

other names: Salmonberry
height: 3 to 5 feet
season: June to July for blossoms,
    July to August for berries

Thimbleberry bushes don't stick you with prickly stems when you sample the berries. Gently pull a berry off the bush and see how it fits over the end of your finger, just like a sewing thimble. Bears love to eat the salmon-pink or white berries, and deer nibble the leaves. Thimbleberries often form thickets that are almost impossible to walk through.

Rubus parviflorus

Blackberry / Red Raspberry

other names: none
height: 3 to 9 feet
season: June for blossoms, July to August for berries

These berries are good to eat either fresh or dried, and birds and animals like them, too. Many people enjoy a cup of tea brewed from blackberry leaves, and the roots are used in some medicines. What a useful plant!

Blackberry
Rubus allegheniensis

Red Raspberry
Rubus odoratus

Conclusion

"Over here! Look at me!" shout the bright colors of a wildflower. The showy blossoms attract us, but more importantly they attract insects and other flying and crawling visitors that pollinate them. Bees, moths, beetles, butterflies, hummingbirds, even ants and bats are essential for wildflowers to make seeds.

When you bend down to enjoy the sweet smell of a fresh blossom, you might share the space with other creatures. Wildflowers may like us to look at them, but they depend upon their other visitors for survival. Remember, if you pick a flower it dies. When you leave it blooming in its own home, the blossom will eventually fade. But its seeds will scatter and provide another year of beautiful wildflowers that you can come back to enjoy. After all, wildflowers always look better in their own homes than in ours.

Glossary

Alternate	Not opposite each other
Annual	A plant that lives for one season
Anther	The part of the stamen containing pollen
Berry	A fleshy fruit containing seeds
Biennial	A plant that lives for two years
Bract	Leaflike scales
Bulb	A plant bud usually below the ground
Corm	A bulblike underground swelling of a stem
Composite	Flower heads composed of clusters of ray and disk flowers
Disk flower	Tubular florets in the center part of a composite flower head
Evergreen	Bearing green leaves throughout the year
Filament	The stalk of the stamen
Floret	A small flower that is part of a cluster
Flower	Part of a plant containing male and/or female reproductive parts
Flower head	A dense cluster of flowers atop a stem
Fruit	A seed-bearing part of a plant
Habitat	The community where a plant naturally grows
Head	A dense cluster of flowers atop a stem
Herb	A seed plant with no woody tissue, whose stems die back to the ground each year
Irregular	Nonsymmetrical in shape
Nectar	Sweet liquid produced by flowers to attract insects
Opposite	Pairs of leaves opposite each other on a stem
Ovary	The part of the pistil that contains the developing seeds
Parasitic	Growing on and deriving nourishment from another plant
Pathfinders	Lines that guide insects to the nectar
Pedicel	The supporting stem of a single flower

Perennial	A plant that lives from year to year
Petals	Floral leaves inside the sepals that attract pollinators
Petiole	The stem supporting a leaf
Pistil	The seed-bearing organ of a flower
Pollen	Powder-like cells produced by the stamens
Ray flower	The flowers around the edge of a flower head; each flower may resemble a single petal
Regular	Alike in size and shape
Rhizome	Underground stem or rootstock
Saprophyte	A plant that lives on dead organic matter
Seed	Developed female egg
Seedpod	Sack enclosing the developed female egg(s)
Sepal	The outermost floral leaf that protects the delicate petals
Shrub	Low woody plant, usually having several stems
Spadix	Fleshy spike that bears flowers
Spathe	Leafy covering connected to the base of a spadix
Spur	Hollow appendage of a petal or sepal
Stamen	Pollen-producing organ of a flower
Stigma	The end of the pistil that collects pollen
Style	The slender stalk of a pistil
Succulent	A plant with thick, fleshy leaves or stems that conserve moisture
Tendril	Slender, twining extension of a leaf or stem
Tuber	A thickened underground stem having numerous buds
Whorl	Three or more leaves or branches growing from a common point

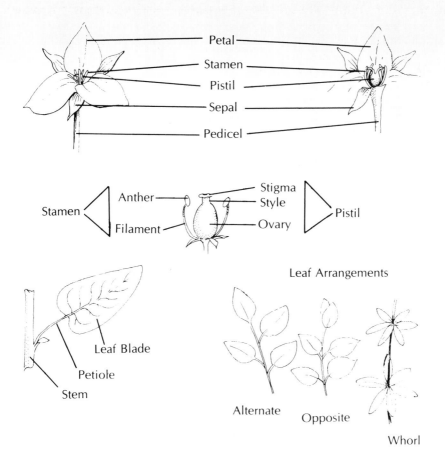

Where to See Wildflowers

Wildflowers can be found anywhere in Minnesota, but some of the best places are parks, forests, nature centers, and recreation areas. Many of these areas have campgrounds, picnic areas, nature trails, and interpretive services to help visitors see and appreciate these lands and their wildflowers. You can get information by contacting the following organizations:

Chippewa National Forest
(218) 335-8600

Voyageurs National Park
(218) 283-9821

Superior National Forest
Boundary Waters Canoe Area
(218) 720-5324

State Parks of Minnesota
(612) 296-6157
There are 66 state parks in Minnesota. Especially nice for wildflowers are: Whitewater, Afton, William O'Brien, Blue Mouns, Lac Qui Parle, Crow Wing, Buffalo River, Itasca, Tettegouche, Lake Bronson, Nerstrand, Fort Snelling, Wild River, Lake Bemidji.

Nature Centers
Wood Lake in Richfield (612) 861-9365
Springbrook (612) 784-3854
Maplewood (612) 738-9383
Dodge (612) 455-4531
Quarry Hill in Rochester (507) 281-6114
Hormel in Austin (507) 437-7519
Wolf Ridge in Finland (218) 353-7414

Nature Conservancy Preserves
(612) 379-2134

Other Opportunities
Eloise Butler Gardens (Minneapolis) (612) 348-5702
Landscape Arboretum (Chanhassen) (612) 443-2460
Minnesota Zoological Garden (Apple Valley) (612) 431-9200
Audubon Center of the North Woods (Sandstone) (612) 245-2648

Index